A User's Guide to the
Book of Common Prayer

Baptism and Confirmation

A User's Guide to the Book of Common Prayer

Baptism and Confirmation

Christopher L. Webber

MOREHOUSE PUBLISHING

Harrisburg, Pennsylvania

Copyright © 2006 by Christopher L. Webber

Morehouse Publishing, P.O. Box 1321, Harrisburg, PA 17105
Morehouse Publishing is an imprint of Church Publishing Incorporated.

Library of Congress Cataloging-in-Publication Data

Webber, Christopher.
    A user's guide to the Book of common prayer : Baptism and Confirmation / by Christopher L. Webber.
    p. cm.
    Includes bibliographical references and index.
    ISBN 0-8192-2214-3 (pbk.)
    1. Episcopal Church. Holy baptism. 2. Baptism (Liturgy)—Texts—History and criticism. 3. Baptism—Episcopal Church. 4. Baptism (Liturgy)—Texts. 5 Episcopal Church. Confirmation. 6. Confirmation (Liturgy)—Texts—History and criticism. 7. Confirmation—Episcopal Church. 8. Confirmation (Liturgy)—Texts.
    I. Title.
    BX5944.B37W43 2006
    264'.0351—dc22

                              2005027310

Printed in the United States of America

06 07 08 09 10 9 8 7 6 5 4 3 2 1

Contents

Part I
Holy Baptism

Introduction

Concerning Holy Baptism

The Bible tells us that Jesus commanded the disciples, "Go therefore and make disciples of all nations, baptizing them in the name of the Father and of the Son and of the Holy Spirit" (Matt 28:19). We also read that when those responding to Peter's sermon on the Day of Pentecost asked "What shall we do," Peter answered, "Repent, and be baptized."

Baptism with water has always been the entrance rite of the Christian Church. Almost from the beginning, there have been different opinions as to who should receive it, how it should be done, and exactly what it means. In recent years, however, there has been increasing agreement among the traditional churches on all these subjects. It is also agreed that baptism with water in the Name of the Father, Son, and Holy Spirit provides membership in the Christian Church and is recognized by other traditional churches.

It is also generally agreed that in a society including people of many other faiths or of no faith at all, it is important that those being baptized and the parents of infants being baptized are instructed in the meaning of baptism and the obligations and privileges that come with it.

In keeping with the insistence of such Reformation leaders as Thomas Cranmer and Martin Luther, we should often remind ourselves of the commitment made in our baptisms. The Prayer Book calls for the renewal of baptismal vows whenever there is a baptism in the church. In any event, the commitment should be revisited at least four times a year: at the beginning of the Epiphany season, at Pentecost, at All Saints, and most importantly at the Easter Vigil.

Baptism is not simply a ceremony marking the beginning of church membership; it is far more radical than that. We begin a lifelong process of growth through which we are united with Christ and given the gift of eternal life. Nothing is more important. The service itself speaks of moving from darkness to light and from death to life. It affects three areas of our lives in profound ways: identity, community, and eternity.

Baptism shapes our identity. Those who are baptized are marked as belonging to God. Baptism is a way of saying that we know who we are: that we are made in God's image and called to belong to God forever.

Baptism creates community. Those who are baptized are embraced by a new community, the church, which is the body of Christ. Baptism is a bond of unity among all those who belong to God.

Baptism gives us life. Those who are baptized acknowledge human mortality and accept the gift of new and eternal life in Christ. In baptism we are buried with Christ and raised to life in him.

To say that baptism also deals with our sinful lives is to say the same things in another way. Sin is separation from God; therefore, we are separated from the source of life, from each other, and even from our true selves. Baptism overcomes that separation and restores us to unity with God, brings us into the Christian community, and restores the image of God in us.

Concerning the Baptism of Infants

Christians have been divided for centuries over the question of whether infants should be baptized. How can infants understand and respond to God's love? One might also ask how infants can understand and respond to a parent's love. The fact is that they do. Love does not require understanding. The tiniest baby can respond to love. As a child grows, she or he comes to understand better what love is, although the wisest theologian can never fully understand. It is not necessary that we understand in order to respond to love.

We know that Jews brought eight-day-old male children to be circumcised and made members of the Jewish community. It would seem likely that the first Christians, coming from the Jewish community, would also have assumed that infant initiation was proper.

There are also indications in the New Testament that infants were baptized by the apostles. There are references, for example, to individuals being baptized "with their household," which would have included children (cf. Acts 16:15 and 16:34).

As with all the sacraments, what matters is not our understanding, which will always be inadequate, but that we bring children to God and deliberately place them in God's loving care.

The introduction to the Confirmation section of this booklet will discuss the process of growth and the mature affirmation of the baptismal promises.

Concerning the Service

The directions on page 298 of the Prayer Book make some important statements, not simply about the service, but also about the nature and meaning of baptism. First and foremost, that through it we receive full membership in the church—a relationship that cannot be dissolved. Baptism, in other words, needs no "completion" in confirmation, nor is there any need for anyone ever to be re-baptized.

Second, baptism is always a corporate act; it involves membership in the church, and therefore the church body should be assembled when there are candidates for baptism. Archbishop Thomas Cranmer stressed this principle in the first English Prayer Book, saying "it should not be ministered but upon Sundays and other holy days, when the most number of people may come together. As well for that the congregation there present may testify the receiving of them that be newly baptized, as also because in the baptism of infants, every man present may be put in remembrance of his own profession made to God in his baptism."

Third, baptism is normally set in the context of the Eucharist, and therefore the shape of the service is that of the first part of the Eucharist. Through much of the church's history, baptism has been ministered either at the Easter Vigil service or as a separate, often private, rite. Now baptism is brought into the center of the church's worship so that all may be reminded of the new life into which we are called.

Finally, adult members of the church are to take responsibility for those newly baptized and see that the promises made in their name are carried out. The role of Godparents should not be seen as an honorary position. Serious commitments are made and should not be made by those unable or unwilling to keep them. If the parents cannot provide such individuals, the congregation may appoint sponsors or Godparents from its own membership.

The "Additional Directions" at the end of the service (pp. 312-13) suggest that the Presentation of the Candidates might not take place at the font and that a procession to the font may instead occur just before the Thanksgiving over the Water. The procession adds a sense of movement from the old life to the new, and a procession to the front of the church after the baptism symbolizes movement into the gathered life of the Christian community.

A candle (often a small replica of the Paschal Candle) may be given to those newly baptized as a symbol of the light of Christ that they will now carry through life.

The Bible and the Early Church

John the Baptist prepared the way for Jesus by preaching a baptism of repentance. The accounts of his ministry and of Jesus' baptism can be found in the four gospels: Matt 3:1-17, Mark 1:1-11, Luke 3:1-22, John 1:19-34.

Jesus often referred to his death as a baptism, meaning a passage through death into life. There is no evidence that Jesus himself baptized but St. Matthew's gospel ends with a command from Jesus that the disciples "Go . . . and make disciples of all nations, baptizing them in the name of the Father and of the Son and of the Holy Spirit, and teaching them to obey everything that I have commanded you." The disciples began to baptize on the Day of Pentecost, when the Holy Spirit came to empower them (Acts 2:37-38). Several other stories of baptisms in the early days of the Church are also recorded.

St. Paul speaks of baptism in terms of the unity it gives us as members of Christ's body (I Cor 12:13 and Gal 3:27-28) and in terms of new life (Rom 6:3-5). There are many sermons from the early days of the Church that focus on baptism, since Lent and Easter centered on the preparation and instruction of new converts. The First Epistle of St. Peter may be such a sermon, and many can be found from Cyril of Jerusalem, St. Augustine, and others.

Holy Baptism

A hymn, psalm, or anthem may be sung.

The people standing, the Celebrant says

        Blessed be God: Father, Son, and Holy Spirit.
People   And blessed be his kingdom, now and for ever. Amen.

In place of the above, from Easter Day through the Day of Pentecost

Celebrant Alleluia. Christ is risen.
People   The Lord is risen indeed. Alleluia.

In Lent and on other penitential occasions

Celebrant Bless the Lord who forgives all our sins.
People   His mercy endures for ever.

The Celebrant then continues

        There is one Body and one Spirit;
People   There is one hope in God's call to us;
Celebrant One Lord, one Faith, one Baptism;
People   One God and Father of all.

Celebrant The Lord be with you.
People   And also with you.
Celebrant Let us pray.

Commentary

The baptismal service begins in the same way as a normal Eucharist. The priest and people greet each other with words appropriate to the season. Since, however, baptism is not recommended for penitential seasons, the third verse and response are unlikely to be used.

The usual opening verse and response are extended with a verse from the Epistle to the Ephesians (4:4–6a), indicating to all that this service will include a baptism or baptisms. The verse also sums up the meaning of baptism: we are brought into one body to share one life as children of one God.

The seven-fold repetition of the word "one" emphasizes the unity we are given in Christ. Jesus prayed at the Last Supper "that they all may be one." We are baptized into one church, not a separate denomination, and God's will for the church is unity.

The Collect of the Day

People   Amen.

At the principal service on a Sunday or other feast, the Collect and Lessons are properly those of the Day. On other occasions they are selected from "At Baptism." (See Additional Directions, page 312.)

The Lessons

The people sit. One or two Lessons, as appointed, are read, the Reader first saying

A Reading (Lesson) from _____.

A citation giving chapter and verse may be added.

After each Reading, the Reader may say

The Word of the Lord.
People   Thanks be to God.

or the Reader may say   Here ends the Reading (Epistle).

Silence may follow.

A Psalm, hymn, or anthem may follow each Reading.

Then, all standing, the Deacon or a Priest reads the Gospel, first saying

The Holy Gospel of our Lord Jesus Christ according to _____.
People   Glory to you, Lord Christ.

After the Gospel, the Reader says

The Gospel of the Lord.
People   Praise to you, Lord Christ.

The Collect of the Day

The beginning of the Eucharist is shortened by omitting the Kyrie or Gloria and proceeding directly to the Collect for the Day. The Collect, or theme prayer of the day, is seldom specifically about baptism (even on the days designated as "appropriate for baptism") unless the baptism is held apart from the Sunday or Easter Vigil service. But all the collects call on God to help us live a Christian life—which is what baptism is all about.

The Lessons

Like the collect, the lessons that follow will be those of the day (unless for very special reasons the baptism does not take place at the Sunday parish Eucharist). Such lessons, however, will not be inappropriate. Since the Bible is the foundation book of the Christian life, there are few passages, if any, that do not bear on the baptized life in some way. The sermon will establish connections between the readings and the baptism, drawing out—for the benefit of all those involved directly in the baptism and the whole congregation—what the lessons tell us about the gift of life that God pours out on the church.

The Sermon

Or the Sermon may be preached after the Peace.

Presentation and Examination of the Candidates

The Celebrant says
The Candidate(s) for Holy Baptism will now be presented.

Adults and Older Children

The candidates who are able to answer for themselves are presented individually by their Sponsors, as follows

Sponsor   I present N. to receive the Sacrament of Baptism.

The Celebrant asks each candidate when presented

Do you desire to be baptized?
Candidate I do.

Infants and Younger Children

Then the candidates unable to answer for themselves are presented individually by their Parents and Godparents, as follows

Parents and Godparents

I present N. to receive the Sacrament of Baptism.

The Sermon

The sermon can be postponed until after the Peace. This provision is probably to allow church school children to leave for instruction after the baptism, but this pattern is less common since giving communion to small children is now usual.

Presentation and Examination of the Candidates

In the usual Sunday service, the sermon would be followed by a recitation of the Creed to express belief in the faith that has been proclaimed in the readings and sermon. When there is a baptism, however, the candidates for baptism are now presented. Baptism expresses in action what the Creed expresses in words.

The candidates are presented by others; even adults do not present themselves. The adult candidate has been instructed by church members who attest to the candidate's faith. In the early days of the church, this process normally took three years. Today many parishes admit candidates for baptism as "catechumens" and assign them sponsors from the congregation to instruct them in the faith over an extended period of time.

Adults are presented first because adult baptism is the normal procedure. Children cannot make the response of faith themselves, so others are delegated to do it for them. In the baptism of adults, the members of the congregation can be especially reminded of the significance of this life-changing act, an act that may not have greatly impacted their own lives if they were baptized as infants.

Adult candidates must also express a desire for baptism. They are not asked to express their faith; they cannot know the full meaning of faith from outside the body of Christ. They can desire it, but they will learn its full meaning only after they are baptized.

When all have been presented the Celebrant asks the parents and godparents

Will you be responsible for seeing that the child you present is brought up in the Christian faith and life?

Parents and Godparents

I will, with God's help.

Celebrant

Will you by your prayers and witness help this child to grow into the full stature of Christ?

Parents and Godparents

I will, with God's help.

Then the Celebrant asks the following questions of the candidates who can speak for themselves, and of the parents and godparents who speak on behalf of the infants and younger children

Question Do you renounce Satan and all the spiritual forces of wickedness that rebel against God?
Answer I renounce them.

Question Do you renounce the evil powers of this world which corrupt and destroy the creatures of God?
Answer I renounce them.

Question Do you renounce all sinful desires that draw you from the love of God?
Answer I renounce them.

Question Do you turn to Jesus Christ and accept him as your Savior?
Answer I do.

Question Do you put your whole trust in his grace and love?
Answer I do.

If an infant is to be baptized, obviously no personal response of faith is possible. Therefore, others must speak on behalf of the child and take on the responsibility of seeing that the child learns to understand and respond to the Christian faith. Godparents and parents are asked to commit themselves to ensure that the child is "brought up in the Christian faith and life" and to pray for the child and witness to the faith by their own lives. When the parents and Godparents have made this commitment, they are in a position to speak for the child.

The next six questions come in two groups: a threefold renunciation of evil, and a threefold commitment to Jesus Christ as Savior. In earlier days, the response to these two groups of questions was sometimes dramatized. The candidates faced the west when they renounced evil and then turned to the east—the place where the dawn breaks with new light and the direction from which it was supposed the Savior would come again—to promise to follow Christ as Lord.

It is worth mentioning that candidates renounce external forces of evil in two of the three renunciations; they renounce the evil within in the last. We live in a society that is increasingly aware of the limits of individual human effort and the way that our best efforts can be undone by powers beyond our control. To say we will not obey those powers is a first step; to join the community in which God's grace is at work is the second critical step toward overcoming the power of evil in our lives.

Question   Do you promise to follow and obey him as your Lord?

Answer   I do.

When there are others to be presented, the Bishop says

The other Candidate(s) will now be presented.

Presenters   I present *these persons* for Confirmation.

or   I present *these persons* to be received into this Communion.

or   I present *these persons* who *desire* to reaffirm *their* baptismal vows.

The Bishop asks the candidates

Do you reaffirm your renunciation of evil?

Candidate   I do.

Bishop

Do you renew your commitment to Jesus Christ?

Candidate

I do, and with God's grace I will follow him as my Savior and Lord.

After all have been presented, the Celebrant addresses the congregation, saying

Will you who witness these vows do all in your power to support *these persons* in *their* life in Christ?

People   We will.

The Celebrant then says these or similar words

Let us join with *those* who *are* committing *themselves* to Christ and renew our own baptismal covenant.

The Order for Holy Baptism also provides an opportunity to present candidates to be confirmed, to be received from another Communion, and to reaffirm their faith. Each of these groups or individuals is asked to reaffirm their renunciation of evil and renew their commitment to Christ.

Confirmation (see pages 413-19) developed in the Middle Ages as a separate stage in the process of Christian initiation. Those who had been baptized as infants were later brought to the bishop to be anointed with oil, a rite that had once been the final stage of the baptismal service itself. Gradually, this rite came to be seen as the completion of baptism and a separate conferring of the Holy Spirit. It also served as an opportunity for candidates to take upon themselves the promises their Godparents had made for them in baptism. Whether this rite still has a separate value is much debated, but it has deep roots in Anglican tradition. (See the further discussion later in the commentary on Confirmation on page 27).

Those who have been baptized and confirmed by a bishop of another church need not be reconfirmed to become members of the Episcopal Church. They are presented to the bishop, who prays for them and welcomes them into the Episcopal Church.

Some candidates are given the opportunity to mark a reawakened faith with a public act of commitment. This is a new provision that has been welcomed as a valuable addition in many parishes.

When all have been presented, the congregation is asked to support the candidates and invited to renew their own baptismal covenant. Their support is vital since those baptized enter into a community sharing a common life. We cannot be Christians alone. Adults who are baptized need to be invited into parish activities, given responsible ministries to carry out, and encouraged to join in Bible study groups and similar activities in which their understanding of the faith can grow and develop.

The Baptismal Covenant

Celebrant Do you believe in God the Father?
People I believe in God, the Father almighty,
  creator of heaven and earth.

Celebrant Do you believe in Jesus Christ, the Son of God?
People I believe in Jesus Christ, his only Son, our Lord.
  He was conceived by the power of the Holy Spirit
    and born of the Virgin Mary.
  He suffered under Pontius Pilate,
    was crucified, died, and was buried.
  He descended to the dead.
  On the third day he rose again.
  He ascended into heaven,
    and is seated at the right hand of the Father.
  He will come again to judge the living and the dead.

Celebrant Do you believe in God the Holy Spirit?
People I believe in the Holy Spirit,
  the holy catholic Church,
  the communion of saints,
  the forgiveness of sins,
  the resurrection of the body,
  and the life everlasting.

Celebrant Will you continue in the apostles' teaching and
  fellowship, in the breaking of bread, and in the
  prayers?
People I will, with God's help.

Celebrant Will you persevere in resisting evil, and, whenever
  you fall into sin, repent and return to the Lord?
People I will, with God's help.

The Baptismal Covenant

This version of the Prayer Book provides a renewed emphasis on the central role of baptism in Christian life. The early church gave it a central place, and the leaders of the Reformation in both England and Germany sought to restore that position. The first English Prayer Book said that baptisms should take place on Sunday to remind all present of their own baptismal commitments. In keeping with that understanding, the whole congregation can renew baptismal promises whenever a baptism takes place.

The Creeds were first developed as baptismal statements and the Apostles' Creed serves as the chief individual profession of faith. As in the early days of the church, the Creed is spoken by the baptismal candidate in response to three questions. The candidate was immersed after each response.

A series of five questions has been added to the Creed, but the only statement of faith made is the Creed itself. The remaining questions deal with the consequences of the Christian faith in daily life. The first question quotes Acts 2:42, which describes the life of the early church and asks whether the candidate will also follow that pattern. The remaining questions move from the continuing need for repentance to the need to proclaim the gospel, to serve others, and to work for justice, peace, and human dignity. The corporate dimension of Christian faith is given appropriate emphasis throughout this Prayer Book. The Christian life is not an individual matter, a "me and God" relationship, but a membership in a body and a life of witness and service. It calls on us to act out our faith in specific ways. It is valuable to be reminded of that whenever there is a baptism.

Celebrant	Will you proclaim by word and example the Good News of God in Christ?
People	I will, with God's help.
Celebrant	Will you seek and serve Christ in all persons, loving your neighbor as yourself?
People	I will, with God's help.
Celebrant	Will you strive for justice and peace among all people, and respect the dignity of every human being?
People	I will, with God's help.

Prayers for the Candidates

The Celebrant then says to the congregation

Let us now pray for *these persons* who *are* to receive the Sacrament of new birth [and for those (this person) who *have* renewed *their* commitment to Christ.]

A Person appointed leads the following petitions

Leader	Deliver *them*, O Lord, from the way of sin and death.
People	Lord, hear our prayer.
Leader	Open *their hearts* to your grace and truth.
People	Lord, hear our prayer.
Leader	Fill *them* with your holy and life-giving Spirit.
People	Lord, hear our prayer.
Leader	Keep *them* in the faith and communion of your holy Church.
People	Lord, hear our prayer.
Leader	Teach *them* to love others in the power of the Spirit.
People	Lord, hear our prayer.

Procession to the Font

If the Presentation of the Candidates does not take place at the font, the clergy, parents, and sponsors may go to the font at this point or after the Prayers for the Candidates. A hymn, psalm, or anthem may be sung during the Procession.

Prayers for the Candidates

The priest now invites the congregation to pray for those who are being baptized or renewing their commitment to Christ. The prayers that follow were composed for this Prayer Book and may be led by one of the Godparents or another friend or relative of a candidate. The pronoun *them* in italics may be changed to *him* or *her*, but might also, if there are not too many candidates, be changed to the names of the candidates, at least in the first petition.

The petitions move logically, like the previous series of questions, from deliverance from sin to witness and service. First, God is asked to *deliver* the candidates from sin and death, then to *open* their hearts, then to *fill* what has been opened, then to *keep* what has been filled. Those who have come this far can then be *taught*, and when they are taught they can be *sent* to others. Then, at last, they can be *brought* into God's kingdom.

Leader	Send *them* into the world in witness to your love.
People	Lord, hear our prayer.
Leader	Bring *them* to the fullness of your peace and glory.
People	Lord, hear our prayer.

The Celebrant says

Grant, O Lord, that all who are baptized into the death
of Jesus Christ your Son may live in the power of his
resurrection and look for him to come again in glory; who
lives and reigns now and for ever. *Amen.*

Thanksgiving over the Water

The Celebrant blesses the water, first saying

	The Lord be with you.
People	And also with you.
Celebrant	Let us give thanks to the Lord our God.
People	It is right to give him thanks and praise.

Celebrant

We thank you, Almighty God, for the gift of water.
Over it the Holy Spirit moved in the beginning of creation.
Through it you led the children of Israel out of their bondage
in Egypt into the land of promise. In it your Son Jesus
received the baptism of John and was anointed by the Holy
Spirit as the Messiah, the Christ, to lead us, through his death
and resurrection, from the bondage of sin into everlasting life.

We thank you, Father, for the water of Baptism. In it we are
buried with Christ in his death. By it we share in his
resurrection. Through it we are reborn by the Holy Spirit.
Therefore in joyful obedience to your Son, we bring into his

The closing collect introduces the theme of death and resurrection. It is easy to forget that baptism involves these concepts if water is simply poured over the individual's forehead—an act that looks like washing and emphasizes the cleansing of sin. Baptism by immersion, though not always practical, is always preferable because it makes it clear that something more radical than washing is involved: the individual is "buried" in the water not merely to be washed of sin, but to die to sin and be raised to a new life in Christ.

Thanksgiving over the Water

Although the early church believed that all water had been sanctified by the baptism of Christ, prayers for the blessing of the baptismal water began to be said very early in the life of the church. By the Middle Ages, prayers and ceremonies over the water had become elaborate, and Cranmer, like the continental reformers, simplified this part of the service. A prayer for the blessing of the water has, however, remained a strong part of the Anglican tradition, and is modeled on the eucharistic prayer.

The traditional prayers for the blessing of the water have, as this prayer does, usually made reference to the many ways in which God has used water to cleanse and renew the world. The waters of creation, the rivers of Eden, the flood, the Red Sea, the water from the side of Christ, and so on, have typically been remembered here. Some of these are mentioned in this prayer, which gives thanks for the water of baptism in which we share Christ's death and resurrection and the gift of the Holy Spirit.

fellowship those who come to him in faith, baptizing them in the Name of the Father, and of the Son, and of the Holy Spirit.

At the following words, the Celebrant touches the water

Now sanctify this water, we pray you, by the power of your Holy Spirit, that those who here are cleansed from sin and born again may continue for ever in the risen life of Jesus Christ our Savior.

To him, to you, and to the Holy Spirit, be all honor and glory, now and for ever. *Amen.*

Consecration of the Chrism

The Bishop may then consecrate oil of Chrism, placing a hand on the vessel of oil, and saying

Eternal Father, whose blessed Son was anointed by the Holy Spirit to be the Savior and servant of all, we pray you to consecrate this oil, that those who are sealed with it may share in the royal priesthood of Jesus Christ; who lives and reigns with you and the Holy Spirit, for ever and ever. *Amen.*

The Baptism

Each candidate is presented by name to the Celebrant, or to an assisting priest or deacon, who then immerses, or pours water upon, the candidate, saying

N., I baptize you in the Name of the Father, and of the Son, and of the Holy Spirit. *Amen.*

Consecration of the Chrism

In Jewish practice, kings and priests were anointed with oil when they were set apart for their offices. Similarly, the use of oil in baptism began very early. The one baptized is joined in the body of those who share the kingship and priesthood of Jesus who is the Christ, the anointed one.

The oil is ordinarily blessed by the bishop at the cathedral during Holy Week and distributed to the clergy at that time for use in baptism. This prayer, then, is usually omitted but is available for use if the bishop blesses the oil when he or she visits a parish.

The Baptism

At one time, Christian names were given in baptism, but the original custom, now restored, was for candidates to be presented by name. It is Christ's name that is given to us in baptism, not our own.

The Prayer Book mentions baptism by immersion first. Long after the Reformation, this practice was altered only if the infant was too weak to endure such exposure. Unfortunately, many churches today have fonts too small for immersion, but newer churches are once again being built with fonts large enough to make immersion possible. Immersion symbolizes the true meaning of baptism: burial beneath the waters and resurrection to a new life.

When this action has been completed for all candidates, the Bishop or Priest, at a place in full sight of the congregation, prays over them, saying

Let us pray.

Heavenly Father, we thank you that by water and the Holy Spirit you have bestowed upon *these* your *servants* the forgiveness of sin, and have raised *them* to the new life of grace. Sustain *them,* O Lord, in your Holy Spirit. Give *them* an inquiring and discerning heart, the courage to will and to persevere, a spirit to know and to love you, and the gift of joy and wonder in all your works. *Amen.*

Then the Bishop or Priest places a hand on the person's head, marking on the forehead the sign of the cross [using Chrism if desired] and saying to each one

N., you are sealed by the Holy Spirit in Baptism and marked as Christ's own for ever. *Amen.*

Or this action may be done immediately after the administration of the water and before the preceding prayer.

When all have been baptized, the Celebrant says

Let us welcome the newly baptized.

Celebrant and People

We receive you into the household of God. Confess the faith of Christ crucified, proclaim his resurrection, and share with us in his eternal priesthood.

If Confirmation, Reception, or the Reaffirmation of Baptismal Vows is not to follow, the Peace is now exchanged

Celebrant The peace of the Lord be always with you.
People   And also with you.

The artificial division between baptism and confirmation distorts the meaning of Christian initiation and creates the idea that confirmation is necessary for full church membership: the water baptism for forgiveness of sin, and confirmation the gift of the Spirit for strength to live a Christian life. But the postbaptismal prayer makes it clear that the Holy Spirit is given in baptism. The gifts of the Spirit listed in the first prayer on page 308 are drawn from an ancient baptismal prayer based on Isaiah 11:2. This prayer is to be said "in full sight" of the congregation; so, if a baptistery is not fully visible to the whole congregation, the prayer is not said until all have returned to the main body of the church.

The sign of the cross is made on the forehead, using oil blessed by the bishop if desired. Marking the forehead is a custom traced back to Judaism: converts were baptized and then marked with the Taw, the last letter of the Hebrew alphabet, as a symbol of the name of God. The sign is like a brand signifying ownership: the one baptized now belongs to God forever.

The congregation welcomes the newly baptized in word and act, inviting the new member to share in its witness and worship. The Peace here has special meaning; in fact, it is quite possible that the Peace first became part of Christian liturgy at baptisms. In the early church, those who were not baptized had to leave the Eucharist before the Peace was shared. Thus the sharing of the Peace is a special privilege of the baptized through which they express their unity in Christ.

At Confirmation, Reception, or Reaffirmation

The Bishop says to the congregation

Let us now pray for *these persons* who *have* renewed *their* commitment to Christ.

Silence may be kept.

Then the Bishop says

Almighty God, we thank you that by the death and resurrection of your Son Jesus Christ you have overcome sin and brought us to yourself, and that by the sealing of your Holy Spirit you have bound us to your service. Renew in *these* your *servants* the covenant you made with *them* at *their* Baptism. Send *them* forth in the power of that Spirit to perform the service you set before *them*; through Jesus Christ your Son our Lord, who lives and reigns with you and the Holy Spirit, one God, now and for ever. *Amen.*

For Confirmation

The Bishop lays hands upon each one and says

Strengthen, O Lord, your servant N. with your Holy Spirit; empower *him* for your service; and sustain *him* all the days of *his* life. *Amen.*

or this

Defend, O Lord, your servant N. with your heavenly grace, that *he* may continue yours for ever, and daily increase in your Holy Spirit more and more, until *he* comes to your everlasting kingdom. *Amen.*

When adults are confirmed, received, or have renewed their baptismal promises, the bishop prays first for those presented that their baptismal covenant may be renewed and that they may be empowered for Christian service by the gift of the Holy Spirit.

In the early days of the church, Christian initiation was one act including water baptism, an anointing with oil, and laying on of hands by the bishop. Over time, these elements were separated and the bishop's laying on of hands came to be seen as a completion of baptism. Today there is general agreement that baptism with water is a complete initiation in itself. It is, however, important that those baptized as infants be given the opportunity to affirm what was done for them when they are old enough to understand. It is also expected that those baptized as adults be presented to the bishop as a symbol of the diocese and the worldwide church to receive the laying on of hands.

There is a fuller discussion of Confirmation, Reception, and Renewal of Baptismal Vows in the following pages where the separate order of service for these actions is provided.

For Reception

N., we recognize you as a member of the one holy catholic and apostolic Church, and we receive you into the fellowship of this Communion. God, the Father, Son, and Holy Spirit, bless, preserve, and keep you. *Amen.*

For Reaffirmation

N., may the Holy Spirit, who has begun a good work in you, direct and uphold you in the service of Christ and his kingdom. *Amen.*

Then the Bishop says

Almighty and everliving God, let your fatherly hand ever be over *these* your *servants*; let your Holy Spirit ever be with *them*; and so lead *them* in the knowledge and obedience of your Word, that *they* may serve you in this life, and dwell with you in the life to come; through Jesus Christ our Lord. *Amen.*

The Peace is then exchanged

Bishop	The peace of the Lord be always with you.
People	And also with you.

At the Eucharist

The service then continues with the Prayers of the People or the Offertory of the Eucharist, at which the Bishop, when present, should be the principal Celebrant.

Except on Principal Feasts, the Proper Preface of Baptism may be used.

The bishop lays hands on the heads of those presented and prays that God will watch over and protect them. He prays that the Holy Spirit will be with them, lead them, and strengthen them to serve.

The sharing of the peace provides opportunity for those who have received the laying on of hands to exchange greetings with their families and members of the congregation. The sharing of the peace is not, however, an exchange of congratulations, but an affirmation of our unity in Christ as we proceed to the celebration of the Eucharist

The Eucharist usually follows the sharing of the Peace. The forms for confirmation, reception, and reaffirmation are provided on the previous pages (309-10) but would come before the Peace if used.

Alternative Ending

If there is no celebration of the Eucharist, the service continues with the Lord's Prayer

Our Father, who art in heaven,
 hallowed be thy Name,
 thy kingdom come,
 thy will be done,
  on earth as it is in heaven.
Give us this day our daily bread.
And forgive us our trespasses,
 as we forgive those
  who trespass against us.
And lead us not into temptation,
 but deliver us from evil.
For thine is the kingdom,
 and the power, and the glory,
 for ever and ever. Amen.

Our Father in heaven,
 hallowed be your Name,
 your kingdom come,
 your will be done,
  on earth as in heaven.
Give us today our daily bread.
Forgive us our sins
 as we forgive those
  who sin against us.
Save us from the time of trial
 and deliver us from evil.
For the kingdom, the power,
 and the glory are yours,
 now and for ever. Amen.

The Celebrant then says

All praise and thanks to you, most merciful Father, for adopting us as your own children, for incorporating us into your holy Church, and for making us worthy to share in the inheritance of the saints in light; through Jesus Christ your Son our Lord, who lives and reigns with you and the Holy Spirit, one God, for ever and ever. *Amen.*

Alms may be received and presented, and other prayers may be added, concluding with this prayer

Almighty God, the Father of our Lord Jesus Christ, from whom every family in heaven and earth is named, grant you to be strengthened with might by his Holy Spirit, that, Christ dwelling in your hearts by faith, you may be filled with all the fullness of God. *Amen.*

Alternative Ending

An alternative ending is provided if, in exceptional circumstances, the baptism is not part of the Eucharist. The Lord's Prayer is included here since it is a part of every Prayer Book service and would be included if the Eucharist does not follow.

The prayer that follows the Lord's Prayer is a shortened version of a prayer found first in the 1552 Prayer Book. It is only here that the concept of baptism as adoption is mentioned, even though it is an image used five times in the New Testament epistles; it refers back to Israel's adoption and forward to our final resurrection, as well as to the action of baptism. We are created in the image of God but we become members of God's own family, the sons and daughters of God, only through baptism, which may be seen, then, as an adoption ceremony.

The final prayer, like the opening dialogue on page 299, draws on the Epistle to the Ephesians (3:15-17), where the Fatherhood of God is mentioned in relation to the family given God's name. This concluding prayer is offered for all those present, that they may be strengthened by the Holy Spirit and that Christ may dwell in their hearts by faith.

Part II
Confirmation, Reception, and the Reaffirmation of Baptismal Vows

Introduction

The process by which individuals enter into a living relationship with God in Christ has changed drastically through the years and has been a matter of bitter disagreement between separated churches. Baptism with water has always been central to this process, but beyond that there are wide differences.

Scholars believe that in the early days of the church, baptism was normally administered at the Vigil before the Easter Eucharist. Candidates for baptism were carefully prepared and then brought to a service during which they were baptized by immersion, anointed with oil, and then brought to the bishop for a laying on of hands. Gradually, a feeling that baptism should not be long delayed led Christians to begin baptizing in the bishop's absence and therefore to omit the episcopal laying on of hands. Bishops began using this omitted step, however, for individuals who had been baptized under emergency circumstances or by schismatic groups, or for restoring the excommunicated to the fellowship. This action was sometimes referred to as "confirmation." By the middle ages, this rite was often expected of everyone baptized as an infant, and in some areas admission to communion was deferred until this had been done. By the time of the Reformation in the sixteenth century, confirmation was included on a standard list of seven sacraments.

During the Reformation, several different patterns emerged. Some of the more radical reformation groups insisted that baptism itself should be deferred until an individual was old enough to make a mature commitment. Confirmation would then be unnecessary. Martin Luther taught that the local pastor could confirm candidates if desired, but it was not necessary. Roman Catholics admitted small children to communion but deferred confirmation until puberty. They did not require confirmation to be administered by bishops.

Anglicans insisted that confirmation must normally precede admission to communion and that it must be administered by a bishop.

As a result of this development, confirmation became a vital rite of passage for Anglicans (and Episcopalians). Most of those who grew up in the church had vivid memories of being presented to the bishop in their early teenage years before they could receive communion. Adult converts from other churches who had not been confirmed by a bishop in the historic succession were also expected to be confirmed. Adults who had been confirmed in the Roman Catholic Church or anointed with oil blessed by a bishop in the Orthodox Church were received rather than confirmed.

In the last half of the twentieth century, this pattern, although re-enforced by nearly five centuries of tradition, came into question. Scholars were more familiar with the life of the early church, and ecumenical discussions fostered a growing agreement that the current practices were neither historical nor logical. Changes began to take place.

First, recognition that baptism provided full membership in the church made it difficult to speak any longer of confirmation as the completion of baptism or necessary for adult membership. Baptized children therefore began to be admitted to communion. This led to questions concerning the meaning of confirmation and the appropriate age for it. The 1979 Book of Common Prayer, published before these questions had fully been resolved, permits the older pattern to continue but opens up the possibility of using confirmation as a much less significant rite albeit with a broader usefulness. It was no longer to be seen as a unique gift of the Holy Spirit, but instead as a mature affirmation of faith made in the presence of the bishop and sealed by a laying on of the bishop's hands.

In the 1979 Prayer Book, therefore, confirmation may mark a coming of age for those baptized in the church, the admission into the church of individuals from other Christian traditions, and a recommitment to the faith on the part of those who wish to return to an active life in the Christian fellowship. This last use of the rite has become a valuable addition to the life of some parishes but is still hardly used or known in others.

Adults coming from other churches may now receive the laying on of hands. Even Roman Catholics, who are often confirmed by someone other than a bishop and whose rite contains no public affirmation of faith, may take this step. So it is valuable for all adults coming into the church to profess their faith before the bishop and receive the laying on of hands.

Confirmation
with forms for Reception and for the Reaffirmation of Baptismal Vows

A hymn, psalm, or anthem may be sung.

The people standing, the Bishop says

          Blessed be God: Father, Son, and Holy Spirit.
People   And blessed be his kingdom, now and for ever. Amen.

In place of the above, from Easter Day through the Day of Pentecost

          Alleluia. Christ is risen.
People   The Lord is risen indeed. Alleluia.

In Lent and on other penitential occasions

Bishop   Bless the Lord who forgives all our sins.
People   His mercy endures for ever.

The Bishop then continues

          There is one Body and one Spirit;
People   There is one hope in God's call to us;
Bishop   One Lord, one Faith, one Baptism;
People   One God and Father of all.

Bishop   The Lord be with you.
People   And also with you.
Bishop   Let us pray.

Commentary

The order of service for Confirmation is essentially the same as the order for the Ministration of Holy Baptism, but, since confirmation is ministered only by a bishop, the form provided here speaks always of the "Bishop" instead of the "Celebrant."

For many centuries, Confirmation was ministered by the bishop when he visited a parish or, on occasion, in the cathedral. It has recently become customary in many dioceses to hold Confirmation services for a group of parishes once a year in each area of the diocese. This enables the bishop to use the visitation to the parish for more general issues concerning parish life and ministry.

The orders for Confirmation, Reception, and Reaffirmation of Baptismal Vows are set, as the Baptismal service is, in the context of the eucharistic liturgy. The service therefore begins in the usual way with the Salutation but continues with the responsive reading from the Epistle to the Ephesians. These verses sum up the nature of our unity in seven key thoughts: there is one Body, one Spirit, one hope in God's call to us, one Lord, one Faith, one Baptism, and one God with whom we are called into a personal relationship.

The service continues with the salutation before the Collect.

The Collect of the Day

People   Amen.

*At the principal service on a Sunday or other feast, the Collect and
Lessons are properly those of the Day. At the discretion of the bishop,
however, the Collect (page 203 or 254) and one or more of the Lessons
provided "At Confirmation" (page 929) may be substituted.*

The Lessons

*The people sit. One or two Lessons, as appointed, are read,
the Reader first saying*

A Reading (Lesson) from _____.

A citation giving chapter and verse may be added.

After each Reading the Reader may say

The Word of the Lord.
People   Thanks be to God.

or the Reader may say   Here ends the Reading (Epistle).

Silence may follow.

A Psalm, hymn, or anthem may follow each Reading.

Then, all standing, the Deacon or a Priest reads the Gospel, first saying

The Holy Gospel of our Lord Jesus Christ
according to _____.
People   Glory to you, Lord Christ.

The Collect

The Collect is the theme prayer of the Eucharist and would normally be the prayer provided for a Sunday or saint's day, but the bishop is given the choice of substituting a special collect for Confirmation. Special collects are appropriate if the services are not principal Sunday Eucharists in parish churches but area gatherings for Confirmation or special services for that purpose in the cathedral.

The Collect for a Confirmation service can be found on page 254.

The Lessons

Like the Collect, the Lessons may be those of the particular Sunday or saint's day, but may also, at the bishop's discretion, be those provided in the Prayer Book for use at a Confirmation. These readings, from the Old Testament, New Testament, and Gospels, speak of our Christian calling to ministry and of the gifts of the Spirit that strengthen us for such ministry.

Although it was thought that the Confirmation service originated when Christians were first given the gift of the Holy Spirit, the church's teaching now is that the Holy Spirit is given in baptism. Confirmation thus is an opportunity to renew the baptismal commitment made, often by others on our behalf, and to seek new gifts of the spirit for a deeper commitment to Christian witness and service.

The biblical references for the readings can be found on page 929 of the Prayer Book.

> The Gospel of the Lord.

People   Praise to you, Lord Christ.

The Sermon

Presentation and Examination of the Candidates

The Bishop says

The Candidate(s) will now be presented.

Presenters I present *these persons* for Confirmation.

or   I present *these persons* to be received into this Communion.

or   I present *these persons* who *desire* to reaffirm *their* baptismal vows.

The Bishop asks the candidates

Do you reaffirm your renunciation of evil?

Candidate   I do.

Bishop

Do you renew your commitment to Jesus Christ?

Candidate

I do, and with God's grace I will follow him as my Savior and Lord.

Presentation and Examination of the Candidates

The role of sponsors in Confirmation is different from that of sponsors in baptism, especially when those being confirmed are adults. Baptismal sponsors are often friends and relations who can help the parents nurture the child in the faith. Sponsors for adults are more likely to be members of the congregation who are assigned the role. Many parishes now have a catechumenate program in which adult candidates for baptism and confirmation are assigned to members of the congregation for preparation. Such persons frequently meet with the candidate over a period of time and share their faith with the candidate both by teaching and by example. They are then able to vouch for the candidate's sincerity and understanding of the faith.

Three types of individuals may be presented: those who are prepared to be confirmed, those who wish to reaffirm their baptismal vows, and those to be received from another communion.

The Examination

When all the candidates have been presented, the bishop asks them to reaffirm their renunciation of evil and renew their commitment to Christ. Both questions are also asked at baptism, but baptismal candidates are asked to make a three-fold renunciation of evil and a three-fold commitment to Christ.

After all have been presented, the Bishop addresses the congregation, saying

Will you who witness these vows do all in your power to support *these persons* in *their* life in Christ?

People   We will.

The Bishop then says these or similar words

Let us join with *those* who *are* committing *themselves* to Christ and renew our own baptismal covenant.

The Baptismal Covenant

Bishop   Do you believe in God the Father?
People   I believe in God, the Father almighty,
      creator of heaven and earth.

Bishop   Do you believe in Jesus Christ, the Son of God?
People   I believe in Jesus Christ, his only Son, our Lord.
      He was conceived by the power of the Holy Spirit
        and born of the Virgin Mary.
      He suffered under Pontius Pilate,
        was crucified, died, and was buried.
      He descended to the dead.
      On the third day he rose again.
      He ascended into heaven,
        and is seated at the right hand of the Father.
      He will come again to judge the living and the dead.

Bishop   Do you believe in God the Holy Spirit?
People   I believe in the Holy Spirit,
      the holy catholic Church,
      the communion of saints,

When the candidates have made these commitments, the bishop invites the whole congregation to express support for the candidates. More so in the case of adults than children, the congregation will provide the supporting community to which the candidate will look for example and guidance. The degree to which the congregation takes this commitment seriously will directly impact those who have expressed a desire to become active Christians.

The bishop then invites the congregation to join the candidates in reaffirming their baptismal promises. The Prayer Book suggests that this be done four times a year. This reaffirmation is a normal part of the baptismal service and has now become a familiar part of the lives of most active members of the church.

The Apostles' Creed is the earliest attempt at a summary statement of the Christian faith and has been used since the earliest times by candidates for baptism. The Creed speaks of the earthly life of Jesus Christ more than anything else, and most especially of his death and resurrection. This is the center of our faith: the statement that Jesus died and rose for us. It is through baptism that we share his risen life and enter into a living and eternal relationship with him as Lord and Savior.

the forgiveness of sins,
the resurrection of the body,
and the life everlasting.

Bishop   Will you continue in the apostles' teaching and fellowship, in the breaking of bread, and in the prayers?

People   I will, with God's help.

Bishop   Will you persevere in resisting evil, and, whenever you fall into sin, repent and return to the Lord?

People   I will, with God's help.

Bishop   Will you proclaim by word and example the Good News of God in Christ?

People   I will, with God's help.

Bishop   Will you seek and serve Christ in all persons, loving your neighbor as yourself?

People   I will, with God's help.

Bishop   Will you strive for justice and peace among all people, and respect the dignity of every human being?

People   I will, with God's help.

Prayers for the Candidates

The Bishop then says to the congregation

Let us now pray for *these persons* who *have* renewed *their* commitment to Christ.

The petitions on pages 305-306 may be used.

A period of silence follows.

As in the baptismal service, the reaffirmation of faith in the words of the Apostles' Creed is followed with a series of additional questions that spell out the meaning and nature of Christian life and witness.

Notice also how the questions ask for a commitment to the life of the church: following the apostles' teaching, sharing in the life of the church, taking part in the Eucharist (breaking of bread) and in worship. The questions then move on to speak of witnessing that life and faith to others and acting in the world to work for justice and peace. Christian faith always has a social significance. We cannot be Christians without changing the world around us.

Prayers for the Candidates

When the Candidates have made their commitment and the whole congregation has renewed the baptismal covenant, the bishop invites the congregation to pray for the candidates. The prayers provided in the baptismal service may be used and it would be appropriate for one or more of the sponsors to lead the prayers. It would also be possible for the bishop to go directly to the prayer on the next page.

Then the Bishop says

Almighty God, we thank you that by the death and
resurrection of your Son Jesus Christ you have overcome sin
and brought us to yourself, and that by the sealing of your
Holy Spirit you have bound us to your service. Renew in
these your *servants* the covenant you made with *them* at *their*
Baptism. Send *them* forth in the power of that Spirit to
perform the service you set before *them*; through Jesus Christ
your Son our Lord, who lives and reigns with you and the
Holy Spirit, one God, now and forever. *Amen.*

For Confirmation

The Bishop lays hands upon each one and says

Strengthen, O Lord, your servant N. with your Holy Spirit;
empower *him* for your service; and sustain *him* all the days
of *his* life. *Amen.*

or this

Defend, O Lord, your servant N. with your heavenly grace,
that *he* may continue yours for ever, and daily increase in
your Holy Spirit more and more, until *he* comes to your
everlasting kingdom. *Amen.*

For Reception

N., we recognize you as a member of the one holy catholic
and apostolic Church, and we receive you into the fellowship
of this Communion. God, the Father, Son, and Holy Spirit,
bless, preserve, and keep you. *Amen.*

The bishop's prayer was written for this Prayer Book, although it is based on older examples. It asks that the candidates may be renewed in their baptismal covenant and sent out with new strength to serve in the ministry God has given them.

The candidates are now ordinarily called to come forward and kneel before the bishop to receive the laying on of hands. Sometimes when the number of candidates is large, the bishop may choose to confirm two at a time, though always speaking the individual names. It is also possible for the candidates to kneel at the altar rail to be confirmed. The Prayer Book does not direct where candidates should be confirmed or whether they should stand or kneel.

For Confirmation

The first form for the bishop to use was introduced in the 1979 Prayer Book and emphasizes the ministry of the person being confirmed. The gift of the Holy Spirit is given to enable the individual to serve God, not simply to nourish personal spiritual growth. The second form provided was used from 1552 until 1979 and is based on forms used in the German church. In this Prayer Book, the word "servant" replaces the word "child" since the emphasis is on a mature commitment of faith.

For Reception

No separate form for the reception of members from another church was in use until the 1979 Prayer Book, though most bishops already had a form that they used. These forms were used for converts from the Roman Catholic or Orthodox Churches, but since baptism is now understood to provide full membership in the Christian Church, the forms are now intended for all baptized adult converts.

For Reaffirmation

N., may the Holy Spirit, who has begun a good work in you, direct and uphold you in the service of Christ and his kingdom. *Amen.*

The Bishop concludes with this prayer

Almighty and everliving God, let your fatherly hand ever be over *these* your *servants*; let your Holy Spirit ever be with *them*; and so lead *them* in the knowledge and obedience of your Word, that *they* may serve you in this life, and dwell with you in the life to come; through Jesus Christ our Lord. *Amen.*

The Peace is then exchanged

Bishop	The peace of the Lord be always with you.
People	And also with you.

The service then continues with the Prayers of the People or the Offertory of the Eucharist, at which the Bishop should be the principal celebrant.

If there is no celebration of the Eucharist, the service continues with the Lord's Prayer and such other devotions as the Bishop may direct.

The Bishop may consecrate oil of Chrism for use at Baptism, using the prayer on page 307.

For Reaffirmation

The form used here is based on Philippians 1:6 and is intended for the reaffirmation of faith by those who have been inactive for a period of time and wish to participate in ministry.

Since the central action of the service is a laying on of hands, the concluding prayer refers to God's hand stretched out to bless and guide God's people. The "hand of God" is a frequent term in the Bible for God's action in human lives. The bishop's hand may be seen as a symbol of that action.

The service then continues with the exchange of the Peace. Those newly confirmed or received are often encouraged to greet not only their families and friends, but other members of the congregation as well.

The service would normally include the celebration of the Eucharist so that those who have received the laying on of hands may be further strengthened by the gift of Christ's risen life. If there is no celebration of the Eucharist, the service would end with brief prayers and a blessing given by the bishop.

Glossary

All Saints Day: November 1, a day when all the departed, especially those known to us and those of special fame, are remembered. Since the lives of the saints begin at baptism, this day, or the Sunday after it, is one of the appropriate times for baptism.

Catechumen, Catechumenate: Candidates for baptism are called "catechumens," that is, persons under instruction. The catechumenate is the period of time during which candidates are prepared for baptism.

Cathedral: The church in which the bishop of the diocese would normally preside unless he is visiting one of the parishes. The name comes from the Latin word *cathedra* or "seat." The bishop's seat, often an ornate chair, is located in the cathedral. Traditionally the cathedral did not have a parish and was always used for diocesan services, but most American cathedrals are simply large parish churches used in place of the traditional cathedral.

Collect: A short prayer expressing a theme of the day or season. The accent is on the first syllable.

Cranmer, Thomas: The Archbishop of Canterbury in the sixteenth century and the man chiefly responsible for the first English Prayer Book of 1549.

Epiphany: January 6, the twelfth day of Christmas, on which the church celebrates the coming of the wise men. The theme of this season is the light of Christ shining out into the world. The first Sunday of the season celebrates Christ's baptism and is therefore an especially appropriate time for Christian baptism.

Font: The vessel in which baptisms take place, often an eight-sided stand holding a basin of water. The eight sides symbolize what Christians have called the "eighth day" of creation, the day on which Christ rose from the dead beginning a re-creation of human life.

Gloria in Excelsis: An ancient hymn of praise used in the Eucharist in festival seasons.

Grace: A free gift of strength enabling us to serve God.

Kyrie: The "Kyrie eleison" ("Lord, have mercy") is an ancient prayer that is traditionally used early in the Eucharist.

Luther, Martin: A sixteenth century German monk whose proposed reforms in the medieval church led to divisions in the church that persist to this day.

Paschal Candle: The special candle lit at the Easter Vigil that burns throughout the Easter season as a symbol of the Light of Christ. The Paschal Candle is usually placed near the baptismal font and is often lit at baptisms and funerals.

Penitence, Penitential Season: Penitence is the sorrow that one should feel for sins. A penitential season is one in which Christians are called especially to remember their failings and seek forgiveness and renewal. Lent is the primary penitential season, but Advent also has a penitential character. The Fridays of the year are penitential days, except those between Christmas and Epiphany and those in the Easter season (cf. Prayer Book p. 17).

Pentecost: From the same root as "pentagon" ("five-sided"), the Feast of Pentecost is a Jewish festival celebrated fifty days after the Passover. It was on that day, approximately fifty days after Easter, that the apostles first received the gift of the Holy Spirit. The Feast of Pentecost and the long season following it call us to remember the gift of the Spirit and our need to follow the Holy Spirit's guidance.

Psalm: An ancient hymn. The psalms used in the Eucharist come from the book of Psalms in the Bible.

Rite, Ritual: A form of words, the words used in a church service. The word "ritual" is often used incorrectly to mean ceremonies.

Sacrament: "An outward and visible sign of an inward and spiritual grace" (Prayer Book, p. 857). Baptism and Eucharist are the principal sacraments, traditional means by which God acts in human lives.

Vigil: A service of watching, held on the evening before a major festival or at other times (some parishes now have a Vigil Eucharist every week). The Easter Vigil is the central service of the Christian Year and an especially appropriate time for baptisms to take place.

For Further Reading, on Baptism in Particular:

Every, George. *The Baptismal Sacrifice*. London: SCM Press, 1959. Looks at baptism in relationship to sacrifice and the Eucharist in history and contemporary society.

Robinson, J. A. T. *The Body*. London: SCM Press, 1952. Not easy reading, but there are few better discussions of what it means to be a member of Christ's body.

Stevick, Daniel. *Baptismal Moments; Baptismal Meanings*. New York: Church Hymnal Corporation, 1988. Covers the history, theology, and meaning of baptism in contemporary culture.

Merriman, Michael W., editor. *Baptismal Mystery and the Catechumenate*. New York: Church Hymnal Corporation, 1990. A collection of essays, practical and theoretical, on various aspects of the catechumenate as it is being rediscovered by various churches.

Meyers, Ruth A., editor. *Baptism and Ministry: Liturgical Studies One*. New York: Church Hymnal Corporation, 1994. A collection of essays on baptism and ministry.